In Time For Lunch

in time for lunch

In Time For Lunch

The Personal Diary and The Official Journal
of Douglas E. Darbyshire
Surgeon-in-Charge of the Young Women
Emigrants sailing in the S.S. Cornwall
from England to Australia, 1898

reproduced in association with
The Library Board of Western Australia

FREMANTLE ARTS CENTRE PRESS

First published 1991 by
FREMANTLE ARTS CENTRE PRESS
193 South Terrace (PO Box 320), South Fremantle
Western Australia, 6162.

Editor B.R. Coffey.
Designed by John Douglass.
Production Manager Helen Idle.

Typeset in Garth Graphic by Faces, West Perth, and printed on
104 gsm Retreeve (recycled) by Lamb Print, East Perth,
Western Australia.

National Library of Australia
Calaloguing-in-publication data

Darbyshire, Douglas E. (Douglas Edward), 1869-1938.
In time for lunch.

ISBN 0 949206 97 0.

1. Darbyshire, Douglas E. (Douglas Edward), 1869-1938 -
Diaries. 2. Cornwall (Ship) - Travel. 3. Ship physicians - Diaries.
4. Women immigrants - Australia. I. Library Board of Western
Australia. II. Title.

610.92

Contents

Acknowledgements

Acknowledgement for permission to publish this diary is due to The National Library of Australia who hold the original diary in their collection; to Mr W.D. Thorn, who donated the diary to the collection; and to Mrs G.D. Andre, daughter of D.E. Darbyshire.

Acknowledgement is also due to staff of The Library and Information Service of Western Australia: to Nancy Lutton who brought a copy of the diary, held by the Library and Information Service of Western Australia, to our attention, to Chris Jeffery for assistance with preparing the work for publication, and to the State Librarian, Lynn Allen, for her enthusiastic support of the project.

Fremantle Arts Centre Press receives financial assistance from the Western Australian Department for the Arts.

Editorial Note

The text of *In Time For Lunch* is, as far as is practicable, a direct transcription from the original handwritten personal diary and the official journal of Dr Douglas E. Darbyshire. These were written as separate documents.

Occasionally, where errors exist, or a reference is unclear, a clarification has been included in the form of an asterisked footnote. The numbered footnotes to the poem by H. Frederick (pages 77-85) are by Darbyshire and appear in Darbyshire's original diary.

The illustrative material appearing in this volume was originally part of Darbyshire's personal diary and was integrated on the same page with the handwritten text. Placing Darbyshire's illustrations on separate pages from the text is the only reorganisation of the diary that has been made for the purposes of publication.

The title appearing on the original diary is 'The Voyage of S.S. Cornwall April 1898' and on the original journal, 'Journal of Surgeon in Charge of Single Young Women Emigrants on board S.S. Cornwall April 1898'. Therefore, the titles on the present work have been produced by Fremantle Arts Centre Press for the purpose of publication.

The Personal Diary
and
The Official Journal
of
Douglas E. Darbyshire

the inspection of stores

The Voyage of S.S. Cornwall

April, 1898

Having been appointed Surgeon in Charge of the Single Young Women Emigrants sailing in the S.S. Cornwall for W. Australia; I commenced my duties on Wednesday April 24th by inspecting the stores, for their use during the voyage.

The inspection took place at the Royal Albert Docks, and consisted of tasting, and otherwise ascertaining the quality of the foods supplied.

The stores having been passed, the next act was the inspection of the drug stores, which one did not taste.

Then came the interesting ceremony of "Signing on" the Ship's Articles, this was performed in the Saloon. I had not my Certificate of registration with me, of which more anon.

On Thursday the inspection of the Emigrants

the horrors of packing

themselves took place, at the Depot 53 Horseferry Road Westminster. The girls came in in single file past 1st Lord and myself and were subjected to a more or less close scrutiny. Only two were rejected.

These preliminaries over and having completed my outfit, I turned my thoughts to pleasure, and went to the Empress Club Dover [illegible] to lunch with the Manners, who were up in town seeing George off to school.

My last evening was spent at home in a quiet and unessential way.

Next morning came the horrors of packing, the less said about which the better. The awful problems as to which article ought to go into which trunk or bag, the maddening mental calculations as to how much room a given article will take, and as to which will be the best way of packing it, and finally all that having been settled, there comes the terrific tussle with the lids and locks. All this must be passed in silence.

At last all is ready, or is thought to be. The cab comes round, the boxes and bags etc. are put

all with one accord turned
upon the Steward

on top, we put ourselves inside, and off we start for the Station, go to London Bridge then another cab to Fenchurch St. where we meet the Pater with three more packages bringing up the total to eleven, and thence by train to Royal Albert Docks.

Having arrived at the Docks, I proceeded to get on board, the fond parents and B.* coming to see me off.

All was in the wildest confusion. The luggage was dumped down anywhere and nobody knew which was his cabin, and everybody wanted what he could not get, a cabin to himself, and each one had some particularly good reason why he should have the pick of cabins in preference to everyone else; and all with one accord turned upon the Steward, who was very nearly worried off his "chump" as the vulgar put it.

He at last referred to the Captain (who was not on board and was not expected for an hour or more).

---

* *Beatrice Isobel Darbyshire, sister to Douglas. See Appendix Three.*

17

the inspection of the Emigrants

The Captain at length arrived and on being appealed to, said he never interfered in those matters and he left it to the Steward, and eventually it was amicably settled amongst ourselves.

One Dr. Frederick, whom I had known at St. Thomas* was one of the passengers, and he and I agreed to share a cabin between us.

Two other passengers Furness and Davis to wit (of whom more anon) shared another, and the boy Apthorp was given a berth to himself on the ladies side.

After my people had said their last "Goodbye" and we had reluctantly torn ourselves apart, I sat down with Frederick and smoked a pipe and wondered when we should have a meal, and it occurred to us both that such a thing might be forgotten in the disorder and hurry and scurry that prevailed.

The Emigrants were all on board, and comfortably housed in their new, and somewhat

---

* St. Thomas's Medical School, Lambeth, London.

close quarters, and so I had nothing else to do but smoke and wonder.

Presently the Captain came along, and I introduced myself to him, whereupon he asked me if I had my Certificate of registration with me, on replying in the negative, he said I must go and get it, as the Board of Trade would not permit me to go to sea without it.

As there was no possibility of the ship leaving her berth before midnight, I started off for Upper-Norwood.

This put the idea of a meal out of my head, until I reached London Bridge, when nature asserted herself, and was assisted by the memory of a very succulent steak I had partaken of there not long before.

So I entered the Restaurant of the S.E.R.* and ordered a steak and then proceeded to the L.B. & S.C.** station to get a much needed wash and brush up, when whom should I meet but Father.

---

*   South Eastern Railway.

** London Bridge and Southwark Cathedral.

21

Journal of Surgeon in Charge of Single Young Women Emigrants on board S.S. *Cornwall*

April 1898

April 29th

The Emigrants 46 in number were all on board at 4.30 p.m. looking well and cheerful. They immediately proceeded to occupy the berths allotted to them, which were all numbered and named. They were soon comfortably settled, and having had their evening meal retired for the night.

His look of surprise could not have been greater had an earthquake rent the ground and swallowed all the hurrying humanity in front of him.

Having partaken of the steak, in which the Father would not join me, I took train to Crystal Palace and reached home about nine, to the great surprise of Russell and Ann, the only inmates.

Mother and Beatrice were out visiting Aunt Wolfe, who was expected to leave for the Continent on the following day.

My Certificate was locked up in a drawer along with my other papers and the key I had delivered to Mother, who had it either with her or locked up out of our reach.

Father came in shortly after I arrived, and he and I and Russell tried various ways of opening the drawer, but without success until Russell hit upon a key which did the trick.

Having possession of the necessary document, I started off for Gipsy Hill, and on the way met Beatrice and Mother, returning from their visit,

April 30th

The Ship left the Albert Dock at 7.30 a.m. and proceeded to Gravesend, where she was detained owing to the Board of Trade inspection of boilers and engines not having been carried out before.

A stoppage was caused in the flow pipe from the W.Cs. owing to one of the Emigrants having thrust a rag down. This caused the water in the Scullery and wash basins to overflow, but only to such an extent as to cause slight and temporary inconvenience. The obstruction was quickly removed, and the overflow dried up.

The Emigrants are in the best of spirits.

and they turned and walked down to the station with Father and myself and saw me off.

I took bus from Victoria to Liverpool St. and thence took train to Woolwich at 12.10.

Spray the 2nd officer of the ship was in that same train, and he piloted me to her, and I may safely say without his guidance I should never have found her.

I had travelled up with Spray from the Docks to the City and he had then told me he would be in that (the last) train, with which it would be possible to reach the Cornwall that night.

Once on board it was not long before I was in my bunk, Frederick already being safely tucked between the sheets.

When I got up the next morning, we were just moving off and I watched through the port-hole, our gliding past the Dock Gates.

By the time I was dressed we were fairly in the river, and steaming gently towards Gravesend, where we understood we should have to wait a few hours.

*a few words of Comfort to forty
Sea Sick girls*

May 1st

The Emigrants are all well and everything is comfortable for them.
There was no muster this morning, as all the ship's arrangements were
upset owing to the expected visit of the Board of Trade officials.

We were all much occupied in looking at the ships and points of interest we passed and so did not take much note of one another.

Having arrived at Gravesend it appeared to the most casual observer that something was amiss. The Captain evidently not too well pleased, hurriedly went ashore, and a settled gloom showed itself in the faces of the officers, and presently it leaked out that Board of Trade survey of our engines and boilers had not been made, and we could not proceed to sea till that was done, which we were given to understand would take several days.

And such proved to be the case, and whilst this delay so near home, and yet so far from it, seemed very vexatious, it gave us all time to get accustomed to our new surroundings and their little inconveniences before the greater evil of mal de mer* was upon us.

The wind was very high most of the time we lay at Gravesend, and had we been outside the river's mouth we must have had a good tossing whilst where we were we lay quite snugly.

---

* Seasickness.

27

The Marine Superintendent

In this time we of the ship's company came to know one another. Firstly there was Frederick, he who shared my cabin, and who was united to me by the bond of brotherhood of St. Thomas. He is giving up medicine, the mental strain of it, being too much for his highly strung constitution, and is going out to W.A. to mine, holding some appointment under a syndicate at home. He is armed with a very learned cooking book on assaying in general, and on the finding and purifying of gold in particular.

He has been to sea before, and poses as an authority on things nautical before us land lubbers. He is always willing, ay anxious to explain matters to us, and what he doesn't know he invents. He has alas at his command a fine selection of nautical phrases, which he lets loose at frequent intervals.

There is a young Engineer named Furness going out with some mining plant, which he is to erect and then return. He is a gentlemanly fellow, most neatly attired and at all times, even in his pyjamas, looks the acme of perfection.

There is one Davis, a delicate youth with dyspepsia, who is for ever dosing himself with

Mr. Forgate,
a worthy old Salt

lacto-peptine and other patent remedies. He has a troublesome cough which he explains is due to a too-long uvula tickling his epiglottis.

He has been in the wholesale clothing line, and knows all about it, and has a good stock of common sense in other matters too. He is going into the timber trade now.

Then there is Apthorp the boy, who like all boys of his age (14) is apt to be cheeky.

This is all the men.

There is one lady a Miss Lefroy, a very nice quiet unaffected gentlewoman, who shows much interest in the Emigrants, and who has worked amongst the poor at home, and is evidently anxious to ameliorate every one's lot, which is cast in less pleasant lines than her own.

There is a little girl of five summers Dora Koeppe by name, who has the charms of her age and no others, and there is the Stewardess, a Miss Sanderson, who looks after Dora, of her I can say nothing but that she is pleasant to the eye.

the bum-boat man

The Captain — Young by name — is one of the best, and the officers Williams — Spray — Howell and Holt are good fellows; as are the Engineers, whose names I have not yet learnt.

The time at Gravesend was a little tedious, the only excitement being at each tide, when we swung, and if we swung towards the nearer shore, we only just missed several other craft — mostly tugs — lying there.

Another little excitement was the arrival of the bum-boat* man who brought off a great many things that we did not want and a few that we did.

The daily papers were always received with joy, though we refused to pay at his first price of 4d we gladly gave 2d.

The Spanish American War was of course the great topic, and our chances of falling in with Spanish Men of War were freely discussed.

Besides these passtimes, we had some visitors

---

*   *A boat used in peddling provisions and small wares among vessels lying in port or offshore.*

May 2nd

The day has passed quietly. The Board of Trade officials measured the Emigrant's quarters, and found the cubic space was 9160 ft., sufficient for double the number of Emigrants we have on board.

The *Cornwall* left Gravesend at 7.30 this morning. I sent a letter to the Agent General, informing him of our delay, and the cause thereof and reporting the Emigrants as all well and in the best of spirits.

The decks were scrubbed this morning.

who cheered us up, and relieved the monotony. These were Mrs Young, the Captain's wife and Frederick's Father and wife, besides the two Board of Trade officials, one fat and one lean, who were with us two days, and the Marine Superintendent, a very melancholy man who seemed to flit about in an aimless manner; he generally appeared mysteriously at meal times, very seldom spoke, and was never seen to smile.

We must not forget the pilot too, one Mr. Fosgate, a worthy old salt who could spin yarns by the score. He bares a remarkable resemblance to "Cocky" the cockatoo on board.

Nothing else of note occurred at Gravesend, excepting that one of the girls fell down the companion and I happened to be standing at the bottom at the time, and I think I came off second best.

At last on Monday May 2nd. at 7 o'clock in the evening, the melancholy man and the fat and lean Board of Trade officials took their departure, the moorings were cast off and once more amidst general rejoicings we began to slowly steam down the river again.

May 3rd

Several of the Emigrants were sea-sick this morning, but the most admirable order was kept, and everything was as pleasant as possible under the circumstances. The Captain had an awning put up over the poop, so that those girls who were able to come on deck, could enjoy the air without getting wet, for there were occasional showers. Later in the day, the majority of the girls were sick, but were well tended, the Matron's arrangements working well.

This evening I pointed out to the Captain the fact that the candles supplied for the lanterns were not long enough to burn all night, he thereupon had an electric light fixed up, which will add greatly to the comfort of the Emigrants.

May 4th

All the Emigrants but four were sick to-day, and though several were very ill, none are seriously collapsed. One or two who seemed lower than the others, were given small doses (two teaspoonfuls) of brandy, which seemed to have a beneficial effect.

The low flat banks of the river, with now and again a little house or church snuggling in amongst a clump of trees looked very picturesque in the twilight, and it was a glorious still evening.

At last we had passed most of the points of interest, and at any rate it became too dark to see them, and so we turned in.

Next morning May 3rd. we passed Eastbourne so close that with the glasses one could distinguish the various buildings, and Beachy Head shone forth in all its glory, revelling in the splendour of the morning sun (ahem). Later in the day, we could just discern the beloved Isle of Wight, and that was our last glimpse of old England.

The next all absorbing business was Mal de Mer. Somehow although at times I felt remarkably uneasy I managed to avert the awful climax of that peculiar malady.

My fellow passengers, or rather my fellow landsmen, for I forsooth am one of this ship's company, suffered more or less, and for several meals there were at least three empty chairs.

May 5th

The pitching of the ship has been less to-day, and the girls on the whole
are decidedly better, and in better spirits. Two rations of arrowroot were
served out to-day, to those unable to eat or retain other food, one at mid-
day, the second this evening, and most of the girls were able to take this
and enjoy it. Four girls were given brandy. Several complained this
evening of being hot, but the temperature was barely 65°F. The
ventilation for the present weather is quite efficient, there are two cowl
ventilators opening through the roof, and three port holes open directly
into the quarters, one on the starboard and two on the port side, besides
one on the starboard side which opens into the Matron's cabin, which is
partially partitioned from the general quarters, and one porthole and
one cowl ventilator opening into the lavatory and water closets. The
companion also serves as an excellent ventilator.

One unfortunate fellow (Davis to wit) sat for hours in one position, restful if not dignified, in the smoke room, his disregarded pipe lying on the table at his side.

My protegés the Emigrants also suffered severely, their quarters being right aft, and thus getting the full benefit of the ship's motion. Out of the forty six only the odd half dozen escaped.

I used to go round early morning, that is for three mornings, and say a few words of comfort to forty sea sick girls, and prescribe a little stimulant for three or four worse than the rest. The Matron accompanied me, and always had an apt word for the sufferers.

I used to feel pretty bad myself at these times and wonder now if it was the very fact of having to help, or appear to help the others that made me keep well.

Three days of this misery, and then we ran into smooth waters and bright skies, and all was once more merry.

The first land we saw after losing sight of the

Ushant

May 6th

The sea was smoother this morning, and all the girls but two (Mary Campbell and Annie Fordham) were able to get on deck, and greatly improved during the day, so that by evening all seemed happy and in good spirits. The temperature of the quarters was 65°F this morning and 67°F this evening.

One girl, Mary Mahon, appeared much depressed and sat away from the others, doing nothing to occupy herself. The Matron reported to me that this girl had responded to the calls of nature in her bunk, she was bathed, and her linen washed, and removed to another bunk, a lower one. She having previously occupied an upper berth. The Matron spoke to the girl about her behaviour, and she promised it should not occur again, and attributed her action to fear of getting out of her berth. Nothing more was said to the girl, as I feared from her depressed condition, an attack of melancholia.

This evening both Campbell and Fordham were better.

May 7th

I carefully inspected the Emigrants' breakfast this morning, and found the food of excellent quality and ample in quantity.

All the girls were on deck to-day, though Campbell vomited once, her condition is much improved.

Mary Mahon has somewhat recovered from her apathetic state of last evening, and my worst fears are greatly relieved. Some occupation in the shape of simple needlework was found for her, and she seemed to take some little interest in her surroundings.

The decks were scrubbed to-day, and the quarters are quite sweet. The temperature was 64°F.

Isle of Wight was Ushant* with its two lighthouses and its precipitous cliffs and cruel rocks with the waves breaking over them, so that the foam was clearly visible to us with the aid of glasses, although we were about seven miles out.

After passing Ushant, we had to rely on ourselves for amusement, for there was nothing to break the monotony but a passing vessel which were very few and far between, or the sight of a whale, of which we saw not a few.

So we started "deck-quoits" and an even better game, which in lieu of a better name I call "deck bowls", two goals are marked out in chalk on the deck, each consisting of three concentric rings. The game is to throw the rope quoits into these rings, the centre one counting 3, the second 2 and the outside ring 1.

Half the numbers of each side stand at either ring, and throw against one another into the other ring, the quoits being marked, so that each side knows its own.

---

* *Ile D'Ouessant, off the north-west tip of France, west of Brest.*

May 8th

The Captain and I had a muster of the Emigrants at 10.30 this morning. All the girls were present, looking well and happy. We then inspected the quarters, which were in good order. The floor of the lavatory is not quite sweet, but only needs scrubbing. The W.Cs. were well flushed.

Service was held at 11 a.m. Nearly all the girls attended. Mary Mahon is much better and taking interest in her surroundings. There is no case of sickness.

The temperature in the quarters was 64°F this morning, and 75°F at night.

May 9th

The Captain and I inspected the quarters this morning and all the bedding was brought on deck and aired and the bottom boards exposed. Arrangements were made for scrubbing the lavatory floor. There are no cases of sickness. M. Mahon I regard as convalescent. The quality of the dinner, which I carefully inspected today was good, and the girls expressed themselves as quite satisfied.

The morning temperature was 70°F and the evening 81°F.

May 10th

This morning the Emigrants had their boxes up, and got out of them what they required for the warmer weather. The girls are all in good health. The gratings were taken up in the lavatory, and floor beneath thoroughly scrubbed; the lavatory is now sweet.

Temperature at 10 a.m. 72°F and 81°F at night.

It is wonderful how exciting this game can become, as one player of each side plays alternately, one quoit may be in good position and the next player with a good shot, knock it away and leave his own in the good position.

We used to play games of 50 up, they were often very close, and most exciting, all the players at one end running over to the other rings to settle a knotty point on the position of the quoits.

On Tuesday May 10th. hearing some faint murmurs of land being in sight, I got up very early (about six) and staggered out into the [   ] and there stood and blinked sleepily at what I took to be a cloud rising out of the horizon. I was about to go angrily back to my bunk, when someone mentioned the name of "Canary Isles" so I returned to my cabin and got a pair of glasses and then examined the cloud, which proved to be land, right enough.

It was the Canary Isles, and just discernible, high up in the clouds was the Peak of Tenerife.

Having feasted my eyes on this for a while I returned much pacified to my bunk, but feeling

May 11th

The quarters in excellent condition.

To-day the matron reported to me that she feared the presence of pediculi in the hair of an Emigrant named Mary Daly. I examined her head and found an abundance of "nits" but no pediculi; the girl's hair was very thick, and as the tresses were covered with nits and almost matted, I cut a good deal of it off. I then had her head thoroughly washed, and rubbed with a solution of perchloride of mercury. I also had her removed from the bunk she was occupying and put her in an outside bunk with an empty bunk between her and her next neighbour. The other girls rubbed their hair with paraffin as a precautionary measure.

Ellen Reidy has been suffering from an abscess of the face, which I opened to-day and dressed with Boracic Lint.

Through the kindness of the Captain, an electric light was put up this evening under the awning over the upper deck.

Temp. 72°F and 81°F.

it rather warm, and hearing the men washing down the decks, Frederick and I decided to have a bath, and so turned out again and got the "bo'sun" to turn the hose onto us.

The weather now became perceptibly warmer, and the sea smoother, so that the passengers already lazy became much lazier; our games of deck-bowls became fewer, and even reading was an effort, so that the main passtime now became sleeping.

Personally I was never able to get to sleep in the day-time, though I made up for it at night, whilst the others were more or less restless.

A couple of days or so later, that is on Friday May 13th. we caught a glimpse of Africa in Cape Verd, which we sighted about 10 a.m.

This of course caused intense excitement, but it was a mere bagatelle to the sensation our first "Grand Evening Concert" in the Emigrants' "reserve" (if I may so call the part of the deck occupied by them).

It was the one topic of conversation for the next two days, and even now (May 18th.) it is still

pulling out teeth

May 12th

The quarters were in good order and quite clean this morning. All in good working order.

Ellen Reidy's face was dressed this morning and is certainly better. She has suffered no pain since the abscess was opened.

Mary Daly's head was again rubbed with Perchloride of Mercury, and I now hope no further trouble will arise from this cause.

The quarters were a little cooler to-day and having a light on deck, the girls were able to stay later in the open air.

Temp. morning 69°F Evening 79°F.

May 13th

The quarters were inspected this morning and all found in good order. There is no case of sickness. Ellen Reidy's face is progressing favourably.

There was a concert on deck aft to-night in which the Emigrants took the principal part.

The temperature this morning was 76°F but had only risen to 80°F this evening.

talked of, though as I shall presently show, even more exciting incidents have still since occurred.

Indeed we seem to live in a constant whirl of excitement, not to speak of pulling out teeth and other little pleasantries.

But to return to the concert at which I had the honour of taking the chair.

It was a great success, although there was no one who could play the accompaniments, and so all the girls who took part had to sing unaided, and very well they did it.

Luckily for me Frederick was able to accompany my humble song, "The Old Folks at Home", otherwise I doubt if I should have got through with it.

The Captain sang too, accompanying himself.

As the weather became warmer the games of quoits and bowls became fewer, and many afternoons were given up to sleep.

One man didn't sleep as he said, but he closed his eyes so that he could think better. One day

May 14th

The quarters in good order. The air between decks is fresh, although the morning temperature was 78°F and the evening 85°F. The Emigrants are keeping well and E. Reidy's face is still progressing.

May 15th

Service was held on the deck this morning for the Emigrants. One or two of the girls are slightly sea-sick again, there being a slight swell.
   Temperature morning 85°F Evening 82°F.

I saw and sketched him as he was "thinking".
It took me some time to complete my sketch, but
I found him an excellent sitter, he never budged
once. Here is the result.

I never heard what was the subject for
contemplation, but it was of an all absorbing
nature. That I can vouch for.

On the 17th. May we were directly under the
sun. It was very curious to see the shadows of
men all round them, and not to one side.
Looking down from the upper deck, I saw a
man walking on the spardeck (the deck below),
and he had a pipe in his mouth. The shadow
of the pipe was thrown on the deck just in front
of him.

We stuck our knives into the deck, and if they
were straight they made practically no shadow
at all. I also noticed that the shadow of the top
bar of the railings round the ship, was thrown
onto the bar below.

It was fairly warm to-day.

My daily routine was to get up anywhere
between 7 & 8, go out and have a splash under

May 16th

The quarters in good condition, the lavatory is difficult to keep quite sweet, but certainly could not be called "insanitary". The ventilation is efficient. "Scoops" were put on the port-holes today, and established a good breeze thro' the quarters. There is no sickness. The girls are in good spirits. The matron gave out some sewing to the girls to-day, which they much appreciated.

Temp. morning 84°F Evening 82°F.

the hose, then air oneself in pyjamas on the upper deck, then dress and have breakfast. After breakfast a pipe and at 10 o'clock go aft with the Captain, and inspect the Emigrants' quarters.

Then I usually had some medicines to make up, or some little surgical procedure to attend to, after which I repaired to the Captain's room, and had a lesson in navigation, and after that till dinner time, I puzzled over the nautical problems, set me by the Captain.

Under this regime the mornings quickly sped.

The afternoons I loafed away, either reading, sketching or gossiping.

Lately I have been busily employed writing a play, which the five gentlemen of the Saloon are to act before the Emigrants next week.

This, the rehearsals and making out pro-grammes for other entertainments keep one's mind and hands fully occupied, and time does not hang at all.

The rehearsals are very funny, the boy Apthorp

The rehearsals

May 17th

The quarters in good condition, the lavatory being quite sweet. There is no sickness, excepting one or two who are slightly sea-sick, and one girl has toothache.

Temp. morning 83°F Evening 81°F.

has the part of a young lady, he expressed a great contempt for girls, and it is very difficult to make him assume their little airs and graces. In one scene he has to embrace his (or her ought it to be?) lover twice, he protested strongly against this, however after much to do, we persuaded him to accept the inevitable, and even to go through the ordeal, showing some other emotion than disgust or contempt.

Meanwhile his Mother falls fainting into my arms, and in the middle of this touching tableau, the husband of the lady in my arms, makes his appearance, and demands peremptorily to be informed what I am doing with his wife. All is explained and ends happily.

So passes the day.

On Sundays, we have boat-muster, each member of the Company standing opposite the boat appointed to him, in case of stern necessity.

That only takes a very few moments and then there is time for a pipe and divine service at eleven, which is held "aft" in the Emigrants' quarters. The Captain read the service and I the lessons one Sunday and we change duties

boat - muster

May 18th

The quarters in very good condition, and the atmosphere sweet. One girl Martha Tennyson who had some old stumps of teeth out yesterday, has been very sick and low to-day. I inspected the dinners to-day, they were very good, and the girls expressed themselves as quite satisfied with their fare.

Temp. 82°F and 80°F.

May 19th

The quarters in good condition. The lavatory quite clean and sweet. The water-closets well flushed. Two of the girls are still sick. Martha Tennyson is better. All the others well and happy.

Temp. Morning 80°F Evening 78°F.

the next, he reading the lessons and I the service.

N.B. In the above sketch, all the men are not put in, partly for want of patience and skill on the drawers' part, and partly to show more of the boats. The men in the foreground are ready for inspection. The men in the background are waiting for the order to fall in. The Captain and mate are settling some knotty point before beginning. Some imperfections in the drawing may charitably be put down to the rolling of the ship.

On the evening of the 17th. day of May, Furness (the passenger engineer) and I were sitting in the Saloon "yarning", when we noticed that there was something unusual in the sound of the engines. We remarked it to one another but sat gossiping.

At midnight we were joined by Howell (2nd. Mate) and Frederick, and they had barely sat down, when we heard the telegraph ring that the engines had been stopped. We all ran out and made our way to the engine room, where however nothing but the standing engines met our curious gaze.

May 20th

The quarters in good condition, the atmosphere good. The girls well.
Grace Kirby, Florence Disley, and Fletcher were vaccinated to-day, in accordance with instructions.
Temp. 80°F and 76°F.

May 21st

The ship was stopped this morning for an hour and a half, in order to repair some part of the machinery. The quarters are in good condition as usual. The health of the girls is excellent. Mary Ann Evans is complaining of cold and cough. She kept her bunk to-day, she has been a little sick.
Morning Temp 78°F Evening 75°F.

May 22nd

Muster of Emigrants, and boat stations was gone through this morning, all the girls but one (M.A. Evans) being present. This took place at 10.30. Service was held at 11 a.m. at which most of the girls were present.
The quarters were in good condition. Mary Ann Evans is slightly better. She kept her bunk till mid-day.
Temp. 72° and 76°.

It occurred to me that the "Girls" being "aft" right over the propeller, might be alarmed at the sudden silence, so I went aft, but there was no disturbance, no sign of panic, so I went back to enquire what the cause of the stoppage was.

It turned out to be one of the feed-pipes to the boilers had burst, and the boilers were not only not being supplied with water, but were actually losing water.

All the engineers turned out, and in fifty minutes the damage was repaired, and the gallant ship resumed her weary course.

There was now a question raised, as to whether repairs would hold good till we reached Fremantle or whether we would have to put into the Cape.

We all longed to see land once more, and all wanted to post letters.

The Saloon suddenly assumed the appearance of an extremely busy office, of some gigantic corporation in the full pursuit of active business. Everybody was writing as if their lives depended on it, and large piles of correspondence lay

Got his Sea-legs on.
Quite enjoys a roll

Getting Serious

Sic transit gloria mari

Saved.
Can't go any further

May 23rd

The quarters in good condition.

One of the Sub-Matrons, Agnes Anderson complained of pain in her side, she kept her bunk all day and turpentine and hot flannels were applied, which gave relief. Evans is better. Ellen Reidy's face is not progressing satisfactorily. The others are well.

Temp 72⁰ and 70⁰F.

May 24th

The quarters clean and well kept.

Anderson is still confined to her bunk, but is improving. The others are now well.

This evening at 6.45, a concert was held for the Emigrants, they themselves taking the greater part in it. Fortunately the weather was such that the concert could be held on deck — it went off well, and all seemed to enjoy it.

Temp. 68⁰ and 66⁰.

May 25th

The quarters in good condition, the lavatory quite sweet, the floor and boarding being well scrubbed and the plumbing accessories working well.

The girls in good health, and cheerful.

Temp 68⁰ and 65⁰.

before each writer. I wrote two sheets myself.

But alas this overflow of energy, if not wasted, was slightly mis-timed for alas we did not put into the Cape, and now (June 3rd.) we are a long way past it (Lat.10.S. Long.43.50E)* and the letters are still in our writing cases.

The next little excitement was the ship suddenly starting to roll in the most uncompromising way. Mal de Mer again made its appearance amongst both passengers and Emigrants, though slightly. Now we had to put on our sea legs.

We now came into the region of birds. Albatrosses, Molly-hawks, Cape-pigeons and Cape doves in great numbers followed the ship, and some sailed gracefully over our heads and looked most disdainfully at us. They were very pretty floating and skimming overhead, turning

---

* *This position cannot be correct as it would place the* Cornwall *north-east of Madagascar and west of modern Tanzania. It is likely that the Latitude and Longitude have been inverted. Lat. 43.50.S. Long.10.E. would place the* Cornwall *approximately 600 kilometres (370 miles) south of Cape Town.*

May 26th

All working smoothly and well. The girls healthy and happy. The boxes were brought out this morning and the girls got out what they want for the approaching cold weather.

Temp. 66° and 62°.

May 27th

The quarters in good condition, the lavatories etc. being well cleaned and quite sweet. Julia Fletcher's vaccination has taken well in one inoculation. Florence Disley's slightly in two inoculations, but Grace Kirby's not at all. The latter has good marks from a previous vaccination. The temperature to-day was considerably higher than it has been the last day or two, and the day has been fine, one or two of the girls felt a little squeamish this morning, but all were well this evening.

Temp 66° morning and evening.

May 28th

The sea was on the beam to-day, and the ship rolling a good deal, and the girls being unaccustomed to the motion, fell about a good deal, and were in danger of hurting themselves, so they were kept below part of the day, and when on deck were kept quiet. The quarters in good condition. The girls health (barring a little sea-sickness) is excellent.

Temp 66° and 56°.

and wheeling and dropping, and apparently ever on the point of turning a summersault.

If I were not myself I should like to be a Mollyhawk flying about without the slightest apparent effort.

On Wednesday June 2nd. my play was produced in the Emigrants' quarters, and proved a great success.

Getting the stage and its various appliances was in itself, if not funny, at any rate amusing. Besides it was really wonderful to see how quickly things could be arranged and what splendid arrangements could be effected in a short time.

The sailor truly is a handy man.

The Captain and I went down to the Emigrants' quarters in the morning and arranged where the stage should be. We then had the Carpenter down, and in a very short time, we (or rather they for I mostly looked on) had rigged up a rope on which hung our curtains, with all the "gear" and "tackle" necessary to haul them to and fro.

May 29th

Service was held as usual this morning in the Emigrant's quarters.
Everything is going on well. I inspected the dinner to-day, as usual it
was a good quality and quantity. The girls are in good health.
   Temp. 64° and 56°.

May 30th

The quarters well kept and tidy. Owing to the inclemency of the
weather, the girls were unable to get on deck to-day, but they were all
happy and contented below, being well provided with various games,
amusements and literature. All are in good health.
   Temp. 62° and 66°.

May 31st

The girls were able to get out onto the deck to-day. The sea is much
quieter, and all the girls are feeling well. The quarters are in good
condition.
   Temp. 62° and 56°.

*That was as much as we could get done then,
for this was the only arrangement that could be
left all day, and not be in the Emigrants' way.*

*Whilst we are waiting for evening to come, I
am going to jump on to June 4th, on which day
we fell in with, and signalled a sailing vessel
lying becalmed, and which I mention here
because I want to draw it before I forget it, and
also because the sea is now fairly smooth, and
there is some little chance of drawing a straight
line.*

This little barque was the Glenesk *of
Aberdeen, sailing for Melbourne, and was out
75 days. She wanted nothing, so having dipped
flags to one another we passed on.*

*To return to the drama. The Emigrants' tea
being over, the Captain and I accompanied by
the Carpenter, and all the passengers but
Frederick, who very wisely kept out of the way,
went down to the quarters.*

*In the twinkling of an eye, a table and two forms
which were securely fastened to the deck, were
whipped up and out of the way. Drop curtain
and side curtains, wings proscenium etc. all*

June 1st

The quarters in very good condition this morning. The girls all well. A dramatic performance was given this evening between decks, which the girls greatly enjoyed.

June 2nd

The quarters in good condition and quite sweet, the lavatory and other sanitary arrangements working well. General health excellent.
   Temp. 64^0 and 66^0.

made out of flags and bits of rope were put up in no time. I mostly stood and looked on and received suggestions from every one, which I believe were all excellent in their way, only unfortunately each suggester was acting on an entirely different plan from any other, so their various ideas would not exactly dovetail.

Everything being now ready, the stage furniture being nailed down; in case the ship should roll, we retired and had our meal.

At 7.45 the curtain went up, and my virgin effort was launched.

I was not taking part in the first act so I stepped forth into the auditorium and saw the play front before the scenes, as well as stanchions ventilators etc. would allow.

The play was well received, the "get-ups" of the various actors was quite sufficient to give a good start to the laughter, which the ungainly actions of the he-actresses served to keep going. At any rate, there was an almost continuous roar of merriment from beginning to end.

After the play; the Captain, who was very

M.D. as Chawdaul.

Mr. S. ATTHORP as Betsy

Mr. H. Frederick as Mr. Bubbijawbs

Mr. G. A. Davis as Mr. Bubbijawbs

Mr. R. L. FURNESS as Squeegee

FARCICAL COMEDY ENTITLED
THE EMIGRANT'S CHOICE
Produced on board S.S. CORNWALL
on Wednesday June 2nd 1891.

June 3rd

The weather decidedly colder to-day, though fine. The girls had to go below earlier than usual, but the atmosphere was quite pure, and the temperature only 59°F at 8 p.m. The quarters are in good order; the girls well and cheerful.

Morning temp. 56°.

June 4th

The quarters in as good order as usual, the girls happy and well; in spite of the cold, the majority stopped on deck most of the day. We bespoke a passing ship, which gave the girls some interest, besides their usual games of swinging skipping dancing and having tugs of war. In the evening between decks all are occupied, some sewing, some playing games and a few reading.

Temp 48° and 56°.

pleased with the play stood a "magnum" in the
Saloon to all the passengers. Various toasts were
drunk.

About a couple of hours after this, the electric
light went out all over the ship and stayed out
all night. I do not insinuate that there could be
any connection between the "magnum" and the
darkness, but mention the fact as an interesting
one, for had it happened a few hours earlier it
would have ruined the play.

By special request the play was given again on
Thursday evening in the Saloon, for the benefit
of the officers, engineers and petty officers, for
whom there was not room in the Emigrants'
quarters on the first night.

It was again well received, and when the
curtain fell, and there were loud cries of "Author
Author" — Heck — I was a proud man that
day.

On Thursday June 9th. about eight o'clock in
the morning we passed about two and a half
miles to the south of the isle "St. Paul's".

This island on which is an extinct volcano, and

June 5th

Boat muster was held at 10.15 this morning. All the girls were present, and fell into their appointed positions with alacrity. All were looking well and happy. Service was read at 10.45 between decks, all the Protestants were present.

Temp. Evening 60°F.

boiling springs, is a "Provision Depot Island" that is a store of provisions is kept on it (I believe by the French Government) for the use of ship-wrecked mariners. Several ship-wrecked crews have from time to time been rescued from here.*

The island is also noted for its lobsters.

When the Captain saw the above sketch of St. Paul's, he immediately said "Where is the Nine-pin Rock?" I said off the page.

"Oh" said he "you must put that in, it is the chief characteristic feature of the island". So I put it in, at the bottom of the page, and it is not at all like the original, being too small, and too near the observer as compared with the main island.

While still in view of the island, the ship was stopped for a while, to rest the engines, and we all improved the shining hour by fishing for Cape Hens, Mollyhawks and Albatross, but am pleased to say without success.

---

* *Ile Saint-Paul is in the Indian Ocean approximately mid-distance between South Africa and Western Australia (Lat.39.S. Long.77.50E.)*

June 6th

The soil pipe from the water-closets got blocked by rags to-day, and the water overflowed into the quarters. It was quickly remedied and the floors washed. The quarters otherwise in their usual good order.

The Matron was far from well this morning and on my advice kept her bunk to-day.

This evening I gave a lecture, a preliminary one to a course on ambulance work.

Temp Evening 62°F.

June 7th

The quarters in good condition. Owing to the weather, the girls had to remain below part of the day and the hatch over the companion had to be closed so that the atmosphere was more stuffy to-night than usual. One of the Sub-Matrons was not very well and kept her bunk part of the day. The Matron is better to-day.

Temp 60°F.

In the foreground of my sketch is seen a passenger fishing with a Mollyhawk smiling at the ruse. A little further "aft" is a very enthusiastic member kneeling on the deck cutting up pork for bait. Further aft still the doctor is seen fixing up tackles for the emigrant girls, one or two of whom are seen fishing, or turning, excitedly about.

On another occasion when we stopped for a while, to tighten up the engines, the Captain put some wine into a bottle corked it up, and put a letter T. on it. The bottle was then fastened to a line and dropped overboard, and allowed to sink about 20 fathoms and then hauled up again. The bottle was then full of water, not wine, and the cork was firmly fixed in its proper position in the neck of the bottle, only upside down, that is the end of the cork which had been uppermost and had the T. on it was now below, next the water in the bottle.

We tried the experiment again, but on the second occasion it did not come off, only part of the wine having escaped, and cork half driven down into the bottle.

After passing St. Paul's things jogged along very

June 8th

The quarters in very good condition. The Matron was not so well again
to-day, so I advised her to keep her bunk. Owing to sprays constantly
washing over the poop, few of the girls ventured on deck. The Sub-
Matron is better.

Temp. 58⁰ and 60⁰.

June 9th

The ship was stopped this morning for an hour while the engines were
tightened up. Miss Monk was still unable to come on deck, but the girls
were well cared for, a lady passenger Miss Lefroy staying with the girls
on deck, and helping to amuse them. A number of the girls (16) were
through the kindness of the Captain, taken over the ship, an excursion
they much enjoyed.

This evening I gave another ambulance lecture to the girls, and some
practice in bandaging.

Temp. 60⁰.

quietly, we got up each day, breakfasted and those who had anything to do, did it, those who hadn't loafed about, read a little, slept a little, smoked a great deal, and grumbled much more, till lunch time, after that they occupied the afternoon as they had done the morning only sleeping rather most.

About five o'clock there was generally a gathering of officers engineers and passengers on the aft part of the spar deck, where we walked up and down a space of some twenty yards like caged beasts. Then tea; then some played cards, some spun yarns, and some played other games.

Every day was so like the other that no one had the faintest idea what day of the week it was and much less the day of the month, and on this many acrimonious disputes and heated arguments took place.

An occasional game of chess, varied with monotony, especially when the players were beginners, then every one proffered advice, and the conquered one would say with much feeling "Well I don't profess to play the whole ship."

June 10th

The Matron is still feeling weak and seedy, but was able to get about a little. Fifteen of the girls were shown round the ship to-day seeing the various points of interest, in which they took a most intelligent interest. This evening I gave another lecture on Ambulance and First Aid.

The health of the girls is good. The quarters in good condition.
Temp. 60⁰.

June 11th

The quarters in good condition. The Matron a little better. I thoroughly examined Annie Fordham who has been complaining of various pains, but found nothing seriously amiss with her. Am giving her and Agnes Anderson iron pills. The third batch of girls (15) were escorted over the ship by the Captain and myself. In the evening the two Sub-Matrons were taken over the Engine room.

Temp. 60⁰.

The Captain, who is always contriving something or other to add to the Emigrants' comfort, or to amuse and entertain them, suggested that we should take the girls over the ship, and show them anything of interest.

Well we took them in batches of 15 and how they did enjoy it; it was a positive pleasure to see them so happy.

The Captain led the van, and I brought up the rear, and kept off the too bold or inquisitive. We took them to see the refrigerating engines, and cold store room, the main deck, upper deck and bridge, wheel-house etc. Indeed any little object, was quite sufficient to arouse their keenest interest.

Having shown them all round, we gave them tea in the Saloon, a treat, the equal of which I dare guarantee very few of them ever had.

That over we marched them back to their quarters, simply bubbling over with excitement and enthusiasm with all they had seen.

The man Frederick, who sleeps in my cabin, and makes it beastly untidy, wrote a poem

*Albatrosses, Molly-hawks,
Cape-pidgeon & Cape doves*

June 12th

Muster was held this morning at 10 o'clock. All the girls were present.
Service at 10.45 between decks. The quarters well kept. Matron slightly
better.

Temp. 56^0 and 60^0.

June 13th

The quarters in good condition. General health good. Matron still
indisposed. This evening I distributed the books providing one to each
girl, the Captain and Chief Engineer being present. Afterwards we had a
few songs and a little music.

Temp. 60^0.

about the voyage, in return for the many little acts of kindness I have shown him, and my longsufferingness (N.B. I have only kicked him out of the cabin twice in six weeks), he has allowed me to copy it.

Here it is

The good ship Cornwall put to sea
One sunny eve in May
And gallantly across the seas
She ploughed her lonely way

Her hull was of the finest steel
Her engines strong and fine
Her brass-work glittered in the sun [1]
Her decks were yellow pine [2]

Her masts and spars were straight and true
Her stays were trim and light [3]
Her funnel was of brilliant red
Her cables, — chains of might

[1]   The brass-work was covered with a layer of yellow paint. That man Frederick has no regard for the truth.

[2]   And they leaked, luckily the man Frederick had the upper bunk and he got the full benefit of it, — but oh — his language.

[3]   Extract from a sonnet he wrote years ago.

Her Captain was a gallant Scot
  His ancestors of yore
With good King Bruce at Bannockburn [1]
  Went gaily to the fore

Her mates were men of sterling mould
  The first had sailed the main
For many years — ere on this ship
  As officer he came

The second, Spray, though short in height
  Was yet a man of muscle
Nor feared the biggest man alive [2]
  At argument or tussle.

The third and fourth mates lived together
  The former by his build
Betokened German ancestry
  And well his post he filled

The fourth by birth a Welshman is
  And daily in a book
Notes down the water served out to
  The sailors and the cook

The engineers are five good souls
  Hailing from North and South
And make the fireman feed with coals
  The furnace's wide mouth.

[1] More poetical licence.
[2] So he says.

78

The chief, who once was nearly wrecked
  Upon an icebergs shores
Keeps warm and snug while Mr. Cook
  Tallies the coal and stores

Yet sleepeth he with half closed eye
  When trouble's in the wind
And we know full well a better man
  T'were difficult to find

A brawny Scot drives full ahead
  Keeping the middle watch
The fourth and fifth when not below
  Play quoits beside the hatch.

Two other engineers have we [1]
  And thanks to their endeavour
Fresh meat have we throughout the voyage
  And ice in hottest weather

The bosun and the carpenter
  Direct the motley crew
Whose clothes have suffered sadly since
  Their last runs pay they drew

The firemen and the trimmers too
  From Canning Town have come
And pace the decks in garments spare
  When their four hours are done

[1] *Refrigerator engineers.*

79

The Steward is a little man
   Whose heart is large and good
And with his staff looks after both
   Our comfort and our food

Two doctors are there on the ship
   The first of whom I speak
Wears glasses having rims of gold
   Under his cap's wide peak

The other "doctor" has each day [1]
   Our bread to bake and he
Though neat and clean as any man
   Has skin of ebony

The passengers on board the ship
   Are varied in their kind
Some of them live in the saloon
   The others are behind [2]

These last are guarded jealously
   Both when they sleep in bunk
And on the deck, by one they know
   As Matron — Miss M. Monk.

To see how well her charge she keeps
   Look on these maidens fair
And you will see upon each face
   Rude health depicted there.

[1] *Ships' cooks are nicknamed "doctor".*
[2] *The Emigrants — whose quarters were "aft".*

A rigid line is stretched between
    These maids — and all the others
For they as Emigrants have left
    Home, country Fathers Mothers

To tell the charms of all these maids
    Were far beyond my pen
The others I will now describe
    Beginning with the men.

One of the four is fair and stout [1]
    An Engineer is he
And chiefly here is noted for
    His sleep capacity

Another rather tends to muse [2]
    Upon a chair all day
Thinking of Jarra wood and things
    In countries far away

The third, a child in years and looks [3]
    Once dressed up as a girl
Since then he stands before a glass
    Trying his hair to curl

[1] R. Furness.
[2] G.A. Davis going to the Jarra Wood Co.
[3] S. Apthorp.

The fourth a man of riper years [1]
Has sailed these seas before
His yarns are the tallest kind
Both of the sea and shore

Attend O Muse! List to my prayer
And grant the boon I crave
Whilst I describe the "Laydye Fayre"
Who dwelled on the wave

She maketh tapestry by day
And readeth books of note
And lends a willing ear to tales
Of ship-wrecked men afloat

Alas; we all have spun such yarns [2]
Of perils in the past
Of agonies in sailing ships
Of life before the mast.

That now when e'er some fact is told
Of days that have gone by
She with a smile upon her face
Winketh the other eye [3]

[1] H. Frederick, the author.

[2] Here the author most unjustly lays his own sins on our
young shoulders.

[3] By no stretch of imagination could one picture to
oneself Miss Lefroy "winking".

82

A little girl is in our midst
Attended by a maid
Both after one said accident [1]
Of toffee are afraid

And here described are all the souls
Who dwell upon the ship
Their deeds I now will e'en describe
Ere they from memory slip

The first few days when out from home
Were I regret to state
By many spent in solitude
While they bemoaned their fate

But soon they all good sailors were
And lost the smack of town
And talked of "knots" and "longitude"
And "running Easting's down"

They paced upon the deck all day
And slept below at night
And substituted bunk for bed
And "starboard side" for right

At quoits they sometimes used to play
And jokes would oft run high
One wore a suit of dungaree
One, once chalked the cocks eye

---

[1] This was a job for me. They both burned themselves
making toffee.

Concerts were held on board the ship
   Under an awning spread
The choruses of "Old King Cole"
   Bid fair to raise the dead

Alas! Midst all these deeds of joy
   Come others, and of those
Came slippings down on oily decks
   And spoiling suits of clothes

Of stolen pipes — of cockroaches
   Of ducklings underdone
The last were sent to — somewhere
   And consumed ere set of sun

Of arguments at breakfast time
   Of beds laid over night
Of subterranean noises which
   Would fill all hands with fright.

And how at meals when all seemed fair
   Some sudden lurch would come
And mingle salt with pineapple
   And chutnee with a bun

But all these perils now are past
   The weary days are o'er
Already in faith's seeing eye
   We sight the longed for shore

But, somehow, now that we have come
   Unto the journey's end
We all begin to feel that we
   Ere long, shall lose a friend

For this good ship has been our home
   For forty days and more
And when we have to say "Good bye"
   All of us will I'm sure

Regret that we from friends must part
   Who have, since we have come
From England's shore, strived hard to please
   From dawn to set of sun

We cannot thank you Captain for
   The kindness you have shown
To us who for a while have made
   Your gallant ship our home

But try and read between these lines
   Words that I cannot pen
Of wishes for a safe return
   Back to your wife again

Long may the Cornwall sail the seas
   In cloud, in storm, in shine
And think of us, who with you sailed
   In days of Auld Lang Syne

H. Frederick
11.6.98

the Captain

June 14th

The quarters in good order. The water closets do not work very well, there is an ample supply of water, but is not well directed into the pan, so that often the soil is not washed away.

The girls are contented and well. This evening we had the bran-pie, which gave the girls much amusement and real pleasure. Everything went off very well, though on account of Miss Monk's indisposition the affair was kept as quiet as possible. Decks holy-stoned* to-day.

Temp. 60º.

June 15th

The floors etc were not scrubbed to-day, as the girls had their boxes out and were busy with them all morning. The bunks were cleaned out this afternoon and the quarters put in good order.

This evening an impromptu concert was got up at which the Saloon passengers were present. The girls presented the Captain, Matron and Doctor with testimonials.

Temp. 60º.

---

* Decks were scrubbed with a soft sandstone — holystone.

And now we are getting near our voyage's end, and everyone is getting a little uneasy about their luggage and each is asking each what articles are dutiable and if the Customs officers are strict and so on.

I rather think that after six weeks inactivity, we are all a little indisposed to make any effort, and view the approaching disembarkation with something akin to alarm.

On the evening of Thursday June 16th. the Captain, Saloon passengers and myself went down to the Emigrants' quarters and the Captain and I were presented with testimonials signed by the Matron Miss Monk and all the girls.

After that we had a right merry evening singing and Frederick read his poem, which was greatly appreciated.

About eleven that night we sighted Rottnest light. I went to bed.

At one o'clock Frederick came and said we were signalling for a pilot. So I turned out of my bunk, and came on deck, and saw a few rockets

June 16th

The quarters were thoroughly scrubbed and cleaned. The general health of the girls excellent. The Matron much better. All in good order.

Temp. evening 64º.

fired off, and some blue lights burned, but as there was no response, and it was rather chilly I turned in again.

Shortly afterwards Frederick said the Pilot was aboard, and the next thing I was conscious of was our lying at anchor just off Fremantle.

I dressed and went on deck about seven o'clock. It was very cold. There was a most glorious sunrise. Such gorgeous colours I have never seen in the sky.

But the land, as I and my fellow ship-mates looked at that awful sandy desert of a place, a silence fell upon us. I don't remember any place that had a more depressing effect on me. My first glimpse of America at Chisapeke* was not inspiriting, but my first glimpse of Australia gave me the dumps, and I was not the only one who experienced that feeling.

Shortly before eight, Dr. Hope and Medical Officer of Health came on board, fortunately I had a clean bill of health to offer him.

---

*   It is likely that this is Chesapeake, Virginia.

*they filed past in answer
to their names*

June 17th

Arrived at Fremantle. Officer of Health came aboard and inspected the
Emigrants. All were well.

He inspected the girls, I reading their names out from the list, they filed past us.

They were all dressed ready to go ashore, though when the actual time for leaving the ship came, I think they were all sorry to go, and not a few (especially the Irish who lifted up their voices and wept) shed tears.

Next the Immigration Officer came on board and once more the girls' names were read over, and once again and for the last time they filed past in answer to their names.

The Immigration Officer then addressed a few words of welcome to Australia to them, and they all passed onto the launch, and we went ashore.

When we "fetched" the wharf, it was crowded with men, who gave three cheers for Old England in good deep voice. I called on the girls to give three cheers for Australia, which they did with spirit. This amused my brother,*who was waiting on the wharf for me, immensely.

---

* *Benjamin Harvie Darbyshire. See Appendix Three.*

There were three or four
ram-shackling old buses, with
the most dreadful scraggy broken
down looking screws of horses

There were three or four ram-shackling old buses, with the most dreadful scraggy broken down looking screws of horses waiting for us, and into these the girls were packed.

There were one or two policemen to regulate the crowd, but their services were not particularly required, for although there was a fair crowd of men on the wharf watching us land, they took but little interest in the business of packing the young ladies into the Chariots.

The Captain, the Agent, the Immigration Officer and I clambered up onto the top of one of these conveyances, and as somebody remarked "You want to be a bally acrobat" to do it.

We then galloped off to the Depot at a pace I did not think the old screws capable of.

The Depot consists of a long row of low cottages, with a compound in front of us surrounded by a most forbidding palisade.

A gate was unlocked, and the forty and six ushered in the gate shut, and the key turned.

I wished them all
well, & was sorry
to say Good-bye.

The good woman who has charge of the Depot now appeared. She had a kindly face, and welcomed the girls with a pleasant smile, and proceeded to unlock a door, which led into a narrow passage, down which she went and unlocked a door on the right.

All this turning of keys was horribly suggestive of gaol.

Into this room which was about 20 ft by 30, and which was newly lime washed, and which was furnished with two wooden forms without any backs, the girls went, and the Captain and I were asked to address them.

The Captain said, "God bless you girls and good bye" and then stealthily wiped a tear from his eye.

I then stepped forward, and addressed a few fatherly words, the drift of which was that if they were good girls they would get on and be happy in their new home. I wished them all well, and was sorry to say Good-bye.

Most of the girls wept, the Irish contingent howled.

the Author

The voyage has been a very quiet and uneventful one. The general health of the 46 Emigrants has been very good and their behaviour all that could be desired. The quarters are ample in size, the cubic footage being 9650 cub ft.; they have been kept clean and tidy. The ventilation is good (a full account is given of it in the Journal). The sanitary arrangements are good, the water supply ample. The water closets have not worked very well, the direction of the water-flow into the pan, not removing the "soil". This did not cause a "nuisance" as the "soil" was not allowed to remain. This can be easily remedied in future by directing the flow of water differently or by making the sides of the pan more sloping or of zinc, to which the soil etc would not stick.

The Matron has been indisposed, but has only had to keep her bunk one or two mornings.

The Captain has taken the greatest interest in the Emigrants, and has done all in his power to make them happy and contented.

The Officers have all behaved in a kindly and gentlemanly spirit, and rendered my position easy and pleasant.

We men then retired, and made our way to the Fremantle Club, where after such trying scenes, we drowned our sorrow in a glass of sherry.

In the mean time Ben had got my luggage through the Customs, and having shaken hands all round he and I started off for Perth, which place we reached in time for lunch.

Appendices

Douglas E. Darbyshire

Biographical notes

Douglas Edward Darbyshire was born in Birkenhead, England, on 21 September 1869, the second son of Edward Darbyshire, a partner in the firm of Darbyshire, McKinnell & Co. of Liverpool, shipowners and merchants trading with South America. Sometime in the 1870s or 1880s the family moved to London and lived at Upper Norwood. Darbyshire studied medicine at St Thomas's Medical School, receiving registration in April 1897.

After his arrival in Perth Dr Darbyshire was, in December 1900, appointed government medical officer at Carnarvon, a port town north of Perth. In 1901 he married Frances Worley at St George's Cathedral, Perth. The couple had become engaged in England shortly before Darbyshire went to Western Australia. Frances Worley was a trained nurse who was the matron of a London hospital at the time of the engagement.

In 1902 Dr Darbyshire was appointed Special Medical Officer for Perth, and later he set up a private practice in Peppermint Grove, a suburb of Perth. The Darbyshires had three children who were all born during the time they lived in Peppermint Grove.

The Darbyshire family returned to England in late 1909, as the Perth climate did not suit Frances. They settled in Lincoln where Dr Darbyshire practiced until his retirement in 1934. He died in 1938.

The Darbyshire Family

Father Edward Darbyshire, born 16 June 1840; father of
Douglas. He was a shipowner and partner in the
firm of Darbyshire, McKinnel & Co, Liverpool.
He died 19 May 1920.

Mother Matilda Downs; mother of Douglas. (No other
information could be found.)

Ben Benjamin Harvie Darbyshire, born 4 March 1866;
elder brother of Douglas. Qualified as a solicitor in
England in 1888 and soon after migrated to
Melbourne, Australia. In 1890 he went to Western
Australia and practiced as a solicitor at the country
towns of Albany, Northam, Kalgoorlie and York,
before establishing a practice in Perth in 1895. He
died 18 May 1945.

Beatrice Beatrice Isobel Darbyshire, born 15 November
1873; sister of Douglas. For many years kept house
for her younger brother Russell. Did not marry. Date
of death unknown.

Russell The Most Reverend John Russell Darbyshire, born
1880; younger brother of Douglas. Archbishop of
Capetown, 1938-1948. He died 30 June 1948.

The Female Emigrants On
The S.S. *Cornwall*

We hereby certify that the Ship *Cornwall* is this day starting on her voyage to Fremantle Western Australia, and that the Agent General's Passengers, consisting of the following persons, are duly on board to proceed in her.

Name	Age	Married or Single	Nationality
Mary J Evans	27	single	
Mary McMahon	20	''	Irish
Alice Bailey	25	''	English
Ellen Reidy	27	''	Irish
Martha K Pearson	17	''	English
June Pearson	22	''	''
Bridget McGrath	19	''	Irish
Bridget Quealey	26	''	''
Grace Kirby	25	''	English
Johanna Harte	24	''	Irish
Helen Bedwell	21	''	English
Louisa Wayne	20	''	''
Elizabeth J Wayne	24	''	''
Ellen Hayward	25	''	''
Mary Anne Storcy	23	''	Irish
Clara Kirby	19	''	English
Maude Kate Bale	20	''	''
Ellen Roper	19	''	''
Agnes D Anderson	28	''	''
Sarah A Rice	19	''	''
Annie Fordham	25	''	''
Margaret O Grady	20	''	Irish
Kate Keeffe	19	''	''

Trade or Occupation	Address
Domestic	5 Church St Pennydan Merthyr Tydfil
''	Kilmore Tulla Co Clare
''	18 Holyoake Road Newington Butts SE
''	Moynoe Scariff Co Clare
''	25 Westfield Park Redland Bristol
''	23 Queens Road Manningham Bradford
''	Rossinure Scarriff Co Clare
''	Kildino Lisdeen PO Co Clare
''	7 Elizabeth Cottages Kew Gardens
''	Moynoe Scarriff Co Clare
''	6 Prince Arthurs Cottages Church Lane Hampste
''	Idridgehay Derby
''	''
''	8 Ash Green Copford Colchester
''	Drumbinnis Kinawley PO Fermanagh
''	Elizabeth Cottages Kew Gardens
''	44 Plympton Road Brondesbury
''	The Childrens Home Enner Road
''	385 Euston Road NW
''	230 London Road Thornton Heath
''	
''	Mitchelstown Co Cork
''	Laccaroo Peakle Co Clare

Name	Age	Married or Single	Nationality
Elisa Ellen Horne	26	single	English
Tyrphona M Millward	26	''	''
Edith Hide	19	''	''
Elizabeth McNamara	22	''	Irish
Martha A Tennyson	23	''	''
Elizabeth MacGregor	19	''	Scotch
Elizabeth A Marr	20	''	English
Florence Bisley	26	''	''
Emily M Leesmore	28	''	''
Julia Fletcher	37	''	''
Mary J Davies	27	''	''
Sophia McMahon	28	''	''
Mary Campbell	20	''	''
Martha Davies	18	''	''
Annie Fanning	22	''	''
Kate E Wood	21	''	''
Agnes McHarry	27	''	''
Mary Daly	18	''	''
Bertha Jesson	19	''	''
Mary Scanlan	26	''	''
Ethel T Smith	25	''	''
Kate Pease	24	''	''
Mary A Lewis	19	''	''

Trade or Occupation	Address
Domestic	72 Albert Street Ramsbottom
"	68 Peashill Rise Nottingham
"	2 Hydney St Eastbourne
"	Mary Villa Ennis Co Clare
"	11 St Bridgids Road Drumcondra Dublin
"	The Pines Elgin NE
"	Amesbury Hall Road Blundellsands Liverpool
"	The Dunes Wanen Rd Blundellsands Liverpool
"	5 Wenlock Terrace York
"	20 Dale St Burnley
"	Oldport Oswestry
"	100 Hall St Southport
"	West House Morningside Asylum Edinburgh
"	Pantybredd Ton-yr-efail Nr Perth Glamorgan
"	Rosemary Square Roscrea
"	Clifton House London Rd Southend
"	50 Witham St Newtownard Rd Belfast
"	Cregg Cranghwell Co Galway
"	10 The Avenue Eastbourne
"	Knockdromin Creagh PO Co Limerick
"	44 Breco St Canton Cardiff
"	88 Ashford Rd Eastbourne
"	13 Elvaston Place South Kensington

The Female Emigrants — Historical Note

The group of women aboard the S.S. *Cornwall* were nominated emigrants whose passage had been paid by the colonial government. They were to be employed as domestic workers. This group was one of at least ten such groups that were brought out as nominated emigrants to Western Australia in the 1890s. Mary Pittman Monk, the matron mentioned in Dr Darbyshire's diaries, was employed on at least six such voyages to escort groups of women emigrants.

Throughout the nineteenth century the emigration of single women to Australia was encouraged by governments, the church, employers and unmarried men. Various organisations, some under official patronage, others purely private, were established in the Australian colonies for the purpose of assisting such women to emigrate.

Apart from the labour shortages in the colonies, other reasons single women were needed was to redress the imbalance between the sexes. For example, in 1841 over eighty per cent of the rural population of eastern Australia was male. It was hoped that the women immigrants would marry and have children, and that the presence of women would have a civilising effect upon the colonies. The immigrants themselves, mostly from poor British and Irish families, were attracted by the prospect of finding work, usually as domestic servants, and many also hoped for an early and advantageous marriage. Daughters of lower middle class families were also brought to Australia as governesses.

Upon arrival in the colonies, the single women usually stayed at female immigration depots while waiting to find a job or a husband. Throughout this history of female emigration to Australia there was much exploitation. There was no basic wage for women and many were given hard, demeaning work. Conditions, particularly in rural areas, were often bad, and many women were mistreated. This included both physical and sexual assault. Some women were forced into prostitution to survive because of poor job opportunities and poor pay.

However, it appears that by the end of the 1890s the situation was generally much improved. This was due in part to the efforts of people like Caroline Chisholm who during the 1840s in New South Wales had been active as a social reformer and a migration and employment agent, and had influenced the government and employers to protect and respect the rights of women immigrants. The latter half of the nineteenth century saw gradual improvements in conditions which probably meant that the female emigrants on the *Cornwall* would have been relatively well provided for compared to many of their predecessors. Certainly Dr Darbyshire's account of their shipboard experiences suggests that the general circumstances of female emigration were much better than some earlier records attest.

A Letter From the Emigrants To Captain Young

S.S. *CORNWALL*

The following letter has been received by Captain Young, of the s.s. *Cornwall,* which arrived at Fremantle from London on Friday last:- "We, the undersigned, on behalf of and at the unanimous desire of the whole of the party of young ladies lately passengers on board your ship, wish publicly to thank you for your great kindness and forethought in providing for our comfort while on board, thus rendering what might have been a tedious and weary journey a pleasant voyage. We further desire to convey our thanks to Dr. Darbyshire for his kindness and attention. Wishing both a prosperous career, we are, etc.- Signed: Edith Hide, Agnes Anderson, and Mary J. Evans."

The *West Australian*, Friday 24 June 1898.